SUNDAY SOLOS

FOR PIANO

PRELUDES, OFFERTORIES & POSTLUDES

ISBN-13: 978-1-4234-0273-2

7777 W. BLUEMOUND RD. P.O. BOX 13819 MILWAUKEE, WI 53213

Visit Hal Leonard Online at
www.halleonard.com

CONTENTS

Note: Many of these arrangements are appropriate for more than one category.

OFFERTORIES

POSTLUDES

ALPHABETICAL LISTING OF SONGS

ALL CREATURES OF OUR GOD AND KING

Words by FRANCIS OF ASSISI
Translated by WILLIAM HENRY DRAPER
Music from *Geistliche Kirchengesang*

COME INTO HIS PRESENCE

Words and Music by
LYNN BAIRD

COME, NOW IS THE TIME TO WORSHIP

Words and Music by
BRIAN DOERKSEN

Moderately slow and driving

HERE I AM TO WORSHIP

Words and Music by
TIM HUGHES

Moderately slow

MAJESTY

Words and Music by
JACK W. HAYFORD

HOLY, HOLY, HOLY

Words by REGINALD HEBER
Music by JOHN B. DYKES

OPEN THE EYES OF MY HEART

Words and Music by
PAUL BALOCHE

With steady drive

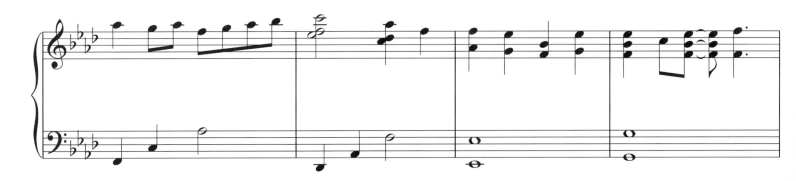

SHINE ON US

Words and Music by MICHAEL W. SMITH
and DEBBIE SMITH

Steadily driving

SPIRIT OF GOD, DESCEND UPON MY HEART

Words by GEORGE CROLY
Music by FREDERICK COOK ATKINSON

WHEN MORNING GILDS THE SKIES

Words from *Katholisches Gesangbuch*
Translated by EDWARD CASWALL
Music by JOSEPH BARNBY

Pensively

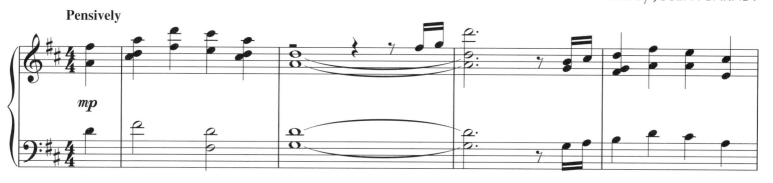

BE THOU MY VISION

Traditional Irish
Translated by MARY E. BYRNE

GIVE THANKS

Words and Music by
HENRY SMITH

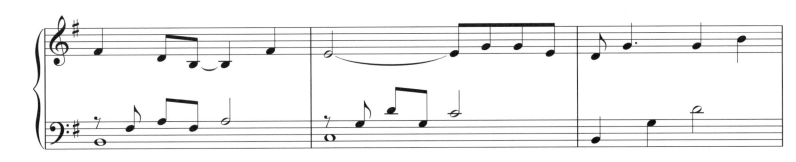

I CAN ONLY IMAGINE

Words and Music by
BART MILLARD

To Coda

D.S. al Coda

CODA

cresc.

f

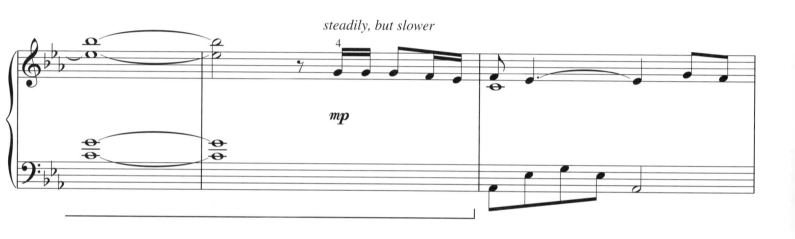

steadily, but slower

I LOVE TO TELL THE STORY

Words by A. CATHERINE HANKEY
Music by WILLIAM G. FISCHER

I WORSHIP YOU, ALMIGHTY GOD

Words and Music by
SONDRA CORBETT-WOOD

Moderately, not too slow

MORE PRECIOUS THAN SILVER

Words and Music by
LYNN DeSHAZO

Warmly

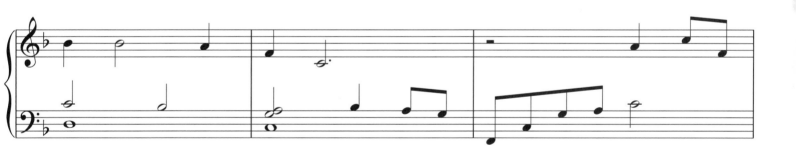

PEOPLE NEED THE LORD

Words and Music by PHILL McHUGH
and GREG NELSON

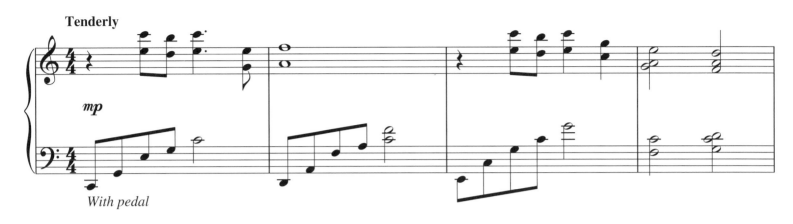

To Coda ⊕

VIA DOLOROSA

Words and Music by BILLY SPRAGUE
and NILES BOROP

Moderately slow

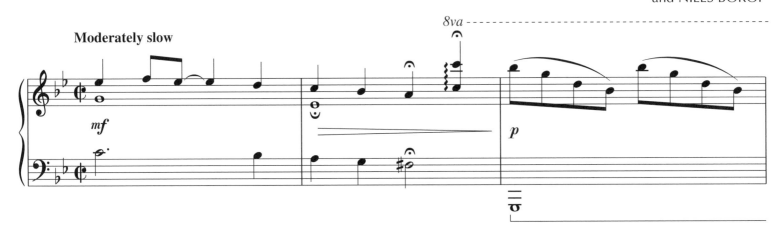

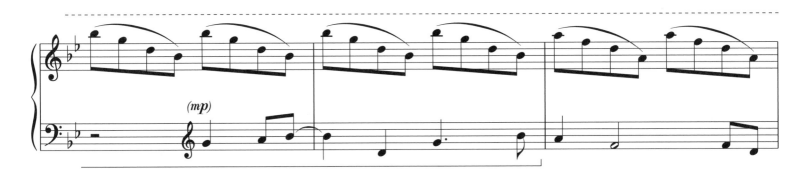

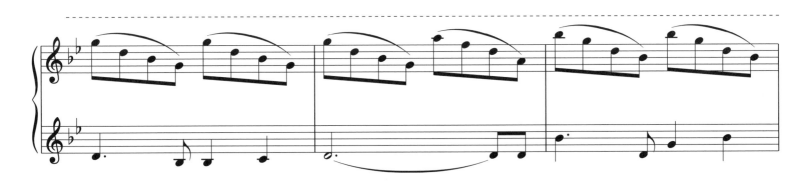

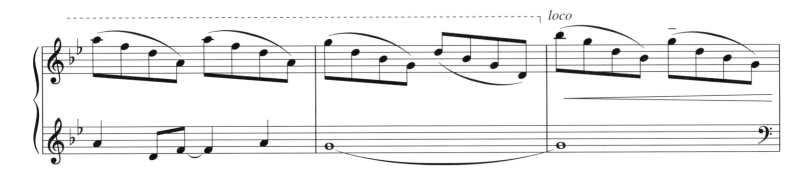

WORD OF GOD SPEAK

Words and Music by BART MILLARD
and PETE KIPLEY

Prayerfully, with reverence

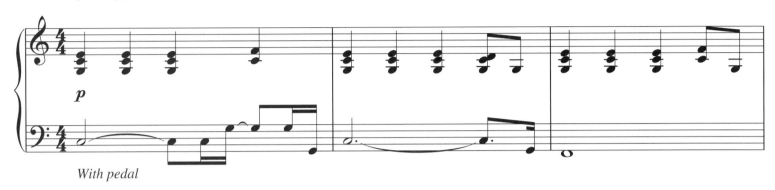

With pedal

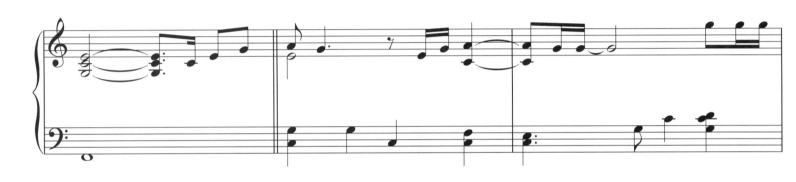

MY TRIBUTE

Words and Music by
ANDRAÉ CROUCH

Moderately slow

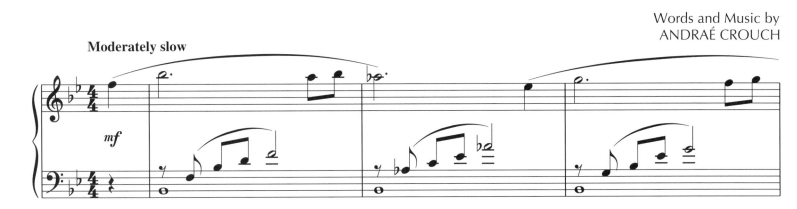

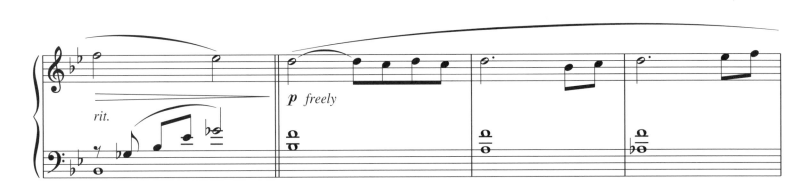

ALL HAIL THE POWER OF JESUS' NAME

Words by EDWARD PERRONET
Altered by JOHN RIPPON
Music by OLIVER HOLDEN

ANCIENT OF DAYS

Words and Music by GARY SADLER
and JAMIE HARVILL

Steady drive

BLESSED ASSURANCE

Lyrics by FANNY J. CROSBY
Music by PHOEBE PALMER KNAPP

Moderate Gospel

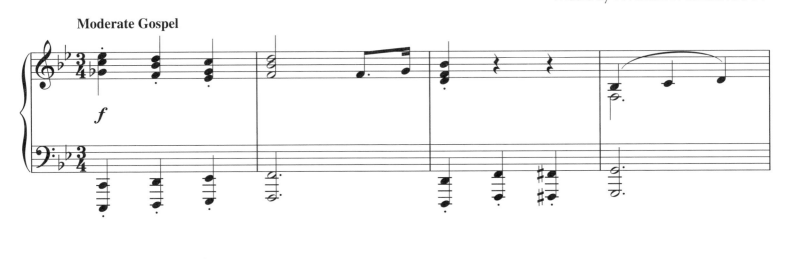

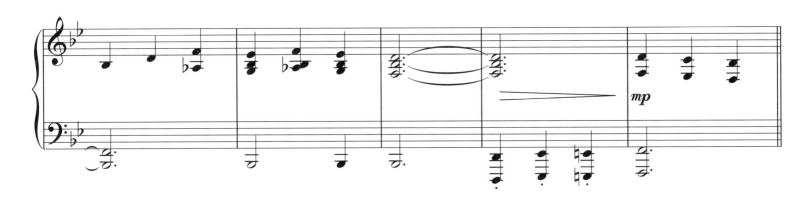

CROWN HIM WITH MANY CROWNS

Words by MATTHEW BRIDGES
and GODFREY THRING
Music by GEORGE JOB ELVEY

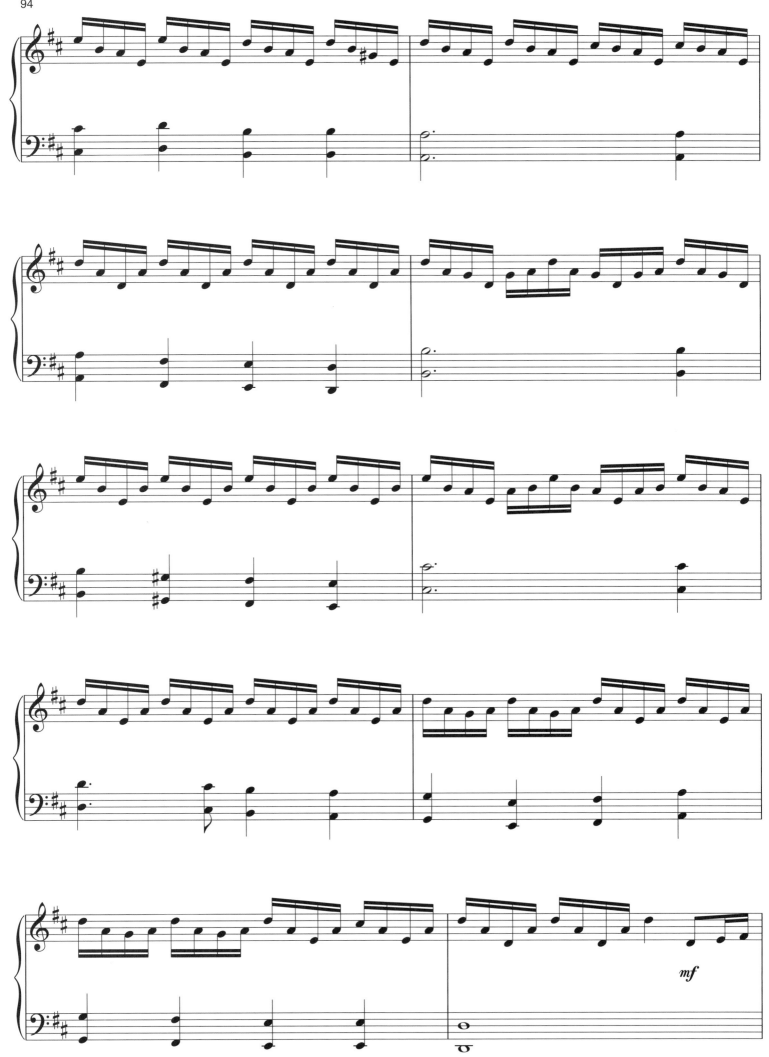

GREAT IS THE LORD

Words and Music by MICHAEL W. SMITH
and DEBORAH D. SMITH

Broadly, not too fast

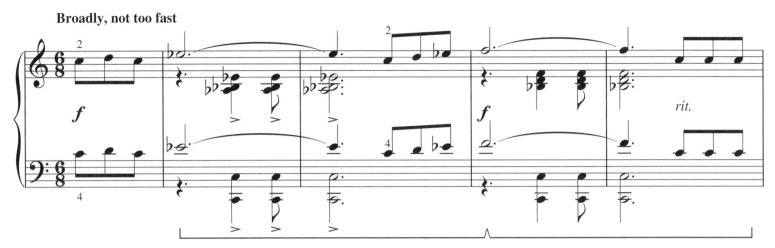

With hushed intensity

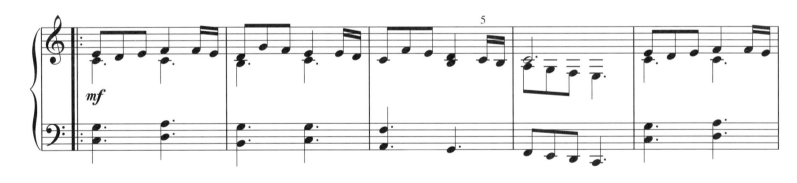

HE IS EXALTED

Words and Music by
TWILA PARIS

SHINE, JESUS, SHINE

Words and Music by
GRAHAM KENDRICK

Moderately

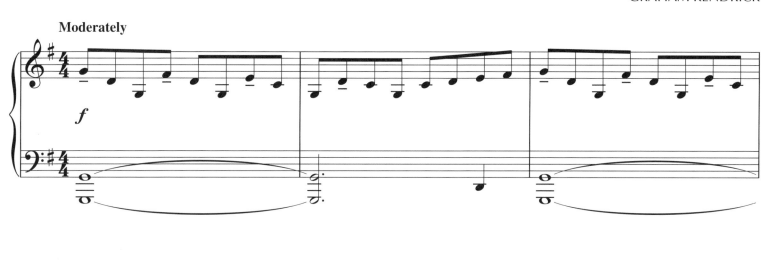

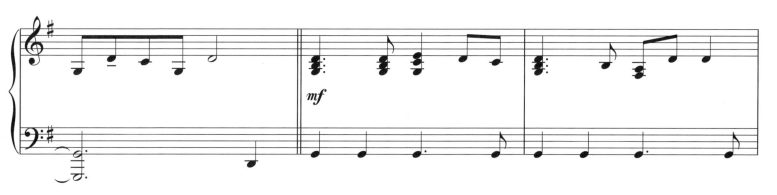

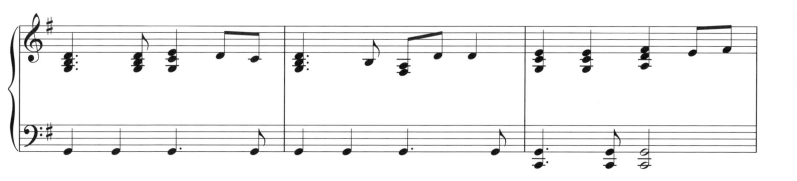

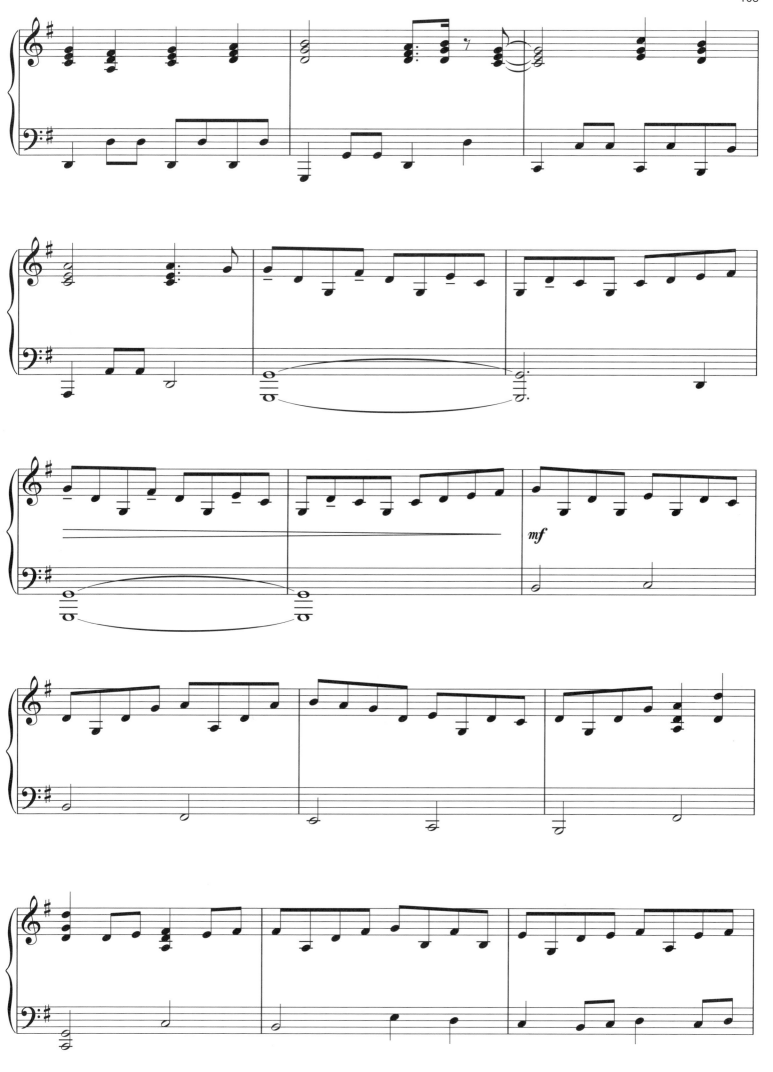

I SING THE MIGHTY POWER OF GOD

Words by ISAAC WATTS
Music from *Gesangbuch der Herzogl*

Triumphantly

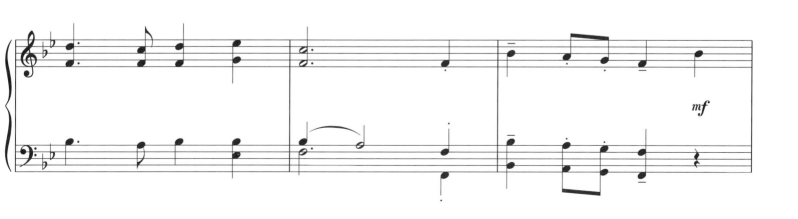

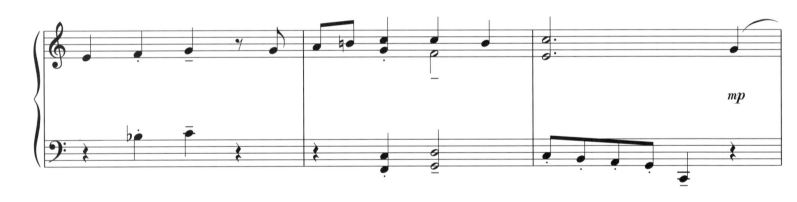

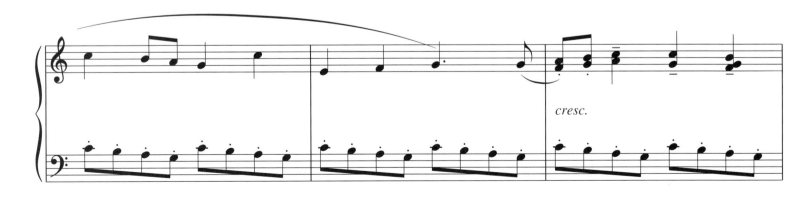

A MIGHTY FORTRESS IS OUR GOD

Words and Music by MARTIN LUTHER
Based on Psalm 46

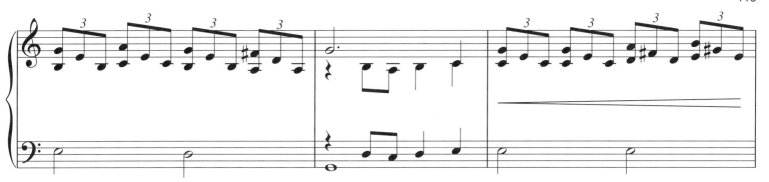

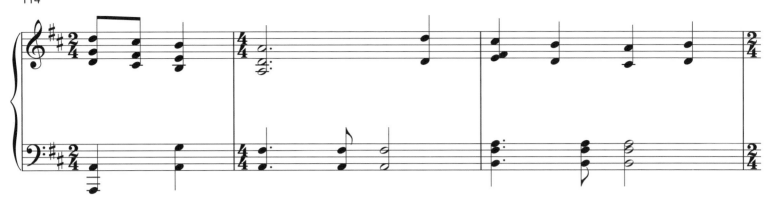

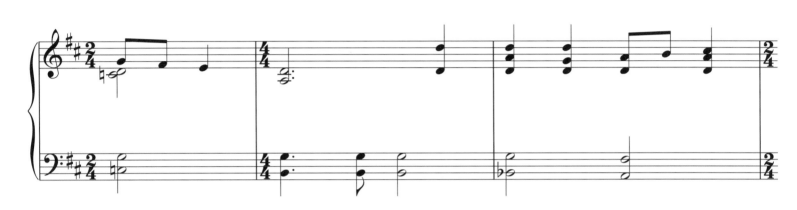

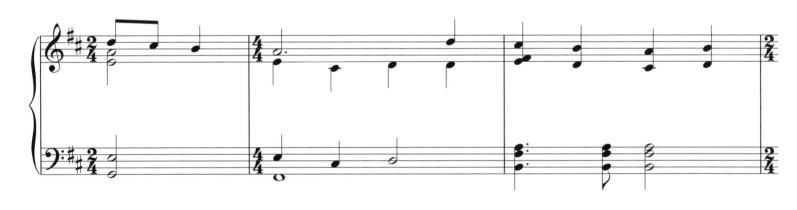

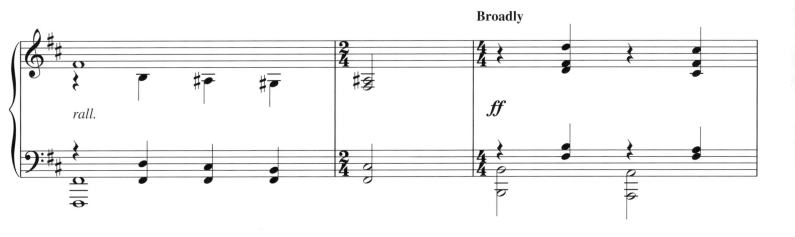

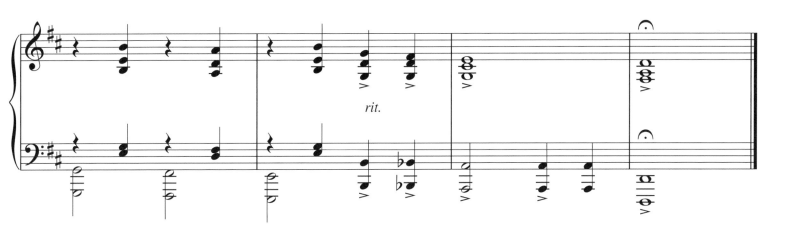

TO GOD BE THE GLORY

Words by FANNY J. CROSBY
Music by WILLIAM H. DOANE

cresc. poco a poco

rit.

Regally, a little slower